The Standout Factor:

The Ultimate Guide to Create a Standout Brand

Taasla Prints

All right reserved. No part of this publication may be reproduced, distributed, or transmitted in any form or by any means, including photocopying, recording,or other electronic or mechanical styles,without the previous written authorization of the publisher, except in the case of brief citations embodied in critical reviews and certain other commercial uses permitted by copyright law.

Copyright © Taasla Prints, 2022

Table of Content:

- CHAPTER 1: Introduction to Branding Yourself ………………….. 6

- CHAPTER 2: Knowing Your Particular Strengths ……………….. 9

- CHAPTER 3: Establishing a Mission Statement ………………….. 11

- CHAPTER 4: Building a Unique Visual Identity ………………. 13

- CHAPTER 5: Establishing an Online Presence 20

- CHAPTER 6: Developing an Interesting Brand Story 24

- CHAPTER 7: Utilising Social Media to Connect with Your Audience 30

- CHAPTER 8: Making the Most of Influencers to Promote Your Brand 33

- CHAPTER 9: Building Relationships at Networking Events 38

- CHAPTER 10: Conclusion 43

CHAPTER 1

Introduction to Branding Yourself

The rivalry for employment, clients, and recognition is getting fiercer every year, and the world is becoming a more cutthroat place. You need to have a strong brand to set yourself apart from the competition if you want to compete in a crowded market. We'll look at the actions you need to follow in this book to develop a powerful personal brand that will make you stand out and be successful.

We'll start by talking about how to identify your special skills and determine your basic values. Then, we'll look at how to construct a mission statement that will direct the growth of your brand and how to design a distinctive visual identity that captures who you are and what you do. We will go through how to use social media and the internet to establish a successful online presence, how to develop engrossing brand narratives, and how to employ influencer marketing. We'll look at the value of networking events for meeting potential partners and consumers in the last section. You need to own all the techniques and tools required for developing a successful personal brand in any business by the end of this book.

CHAPTER 2

Knowing Your Particular Strengths

Your distinctive abilities and ideals should serve as the foundation of your personal brand. Consider what sets you apart from other experts in your sector before starting the process of developing your brand. What unique abilities or character traits do you bring to the table? What would compel consumers to use your services or buy your goods? Understanding these traits can help you create a mission statement and visual identity for your business.

Think about asking yourself things like: What makes me unique in my field? What desires fuel me? What kinds of objectives do I pursue? You may learn a great deal about your own identity by carefully considering these questions, and this knowledge will help you create your unique brand.

Once you have determined some of your special talents, it is critical to successfully express them by developing a mission statement that succinctly captures who you are and what you do.

CHAPTER 3

Establishing a Mission Statement

A mission statement is a succinct phrase or sentence that expresses your identity and what distinguishes you from the competitors. It needs to be impactful and unforgettable. When a potential client or employer reads your mission statement, you want them to know exactly who you are. Here are a few instances of strong mission statements:

- "Creating inclusive, uplifting digital experiences" (Technology firm)

- "Storytelling with creativity to inspire others" (Content creator)

- "Assisting entrepreneurs with data-driven solutions to succeed" (Consultant)

- "Utilising sustainable principles to redefine premium fashion" (Designer of apparel)

CHAPTER 4

Building a Unique Visual Identity

It's the Instagram era right now. More than ever, your success depends on how your brand is seen. The most prosperous firms have thought carefully about or spent a lot of money developing a visual identity.

However, just because billion-dollar firms like Uber are well-known for publishing their visual identity guidelines doesn't imply that younger and smaller organisations can't replicate the key elements of a successful guide on a budget. Small, direct-to-consumer firms may also create their own visual identities at a reasonable price, unlike large corporations. Even if you're just starting off, we advise developing a strong visual identity.

An assortment of components, including your logo, colours, and fonts, creates your visual identity and aids in brand recognition.

BRAND IDENTITY

Vs

VISUAL IDENTITY

You may think of your visual identity as a part of your brand identity. While a brand's identity concentrates on many different aspects, such as design, communications, products/services, and marketing, its visual identity only concentrates on design elements.

The purpose and vision statement, brand story, communication style, and visual identity all fall under the category of brand identity, which is often thought of as the brand's overall direction. The visual identity, on the other hand, is purely concerned with the visual elements of the brand and applies to the website, promotional items, and goods or services.

Building a Unique visual identity requires:

1. Being aware of your audience: Choose a certain audience to which you wish to appeal. Based on your existing social media following or website traffic, demographic information such as gender, age group, and geography may be acquired.

When creating your visual identity, you may then research your audience's habits, activities, and motives more thoroughly.

2. Have a clear objective: A defined mission is vital for your visual identity as well as for business strategy and product design.

An illustration of this is the popular Australian mattress company Koala. They have a delightfully straightforward goal: to promote the health of the environment. In a smart play on their product—mattresses that enhance a home environment—the word "habitats" relates to their focus on sustainability and the environment.

3. Consistency: Is your visual identity consistent across all platforms with your

communication style? The visual identity is consistently consistent throughout all of the samples we've provided, whether you're looking at the brand's website, shop, or Facebook page.

The purpose of developing a visual identity is to assist in communicating your desired brand and messaging by providing a rigid design guideline. Give your visual identity guide to outside aid, such as independent graphic designers, photographers, illustrators, and website designers, to ensure uniformity. When organising and assessing work with independent contractors, always refer to it.

4. Stand out: A strong visual identity may make your business more recognizable. Is my brand easily recognizable? is one thing to consider.

Will potential buyers be able to identify a photo from your business without clicking on the image itself if they see it in Instagram's Explore section?

CHAPTER 5

Establishing an Online Presence

We discovered that nothing is definite when it comes to small enterprises. Businesses have changed, business models have been upended, and consumer habits and behaviours have changed. Adopting new technology and embracing digital methods played a large part in many of these improvements.

Let's now look at how using digital tactics may assist you in creating a strong online presence, connecting with more new clients, strengthening bonds with your current clientele, and raising the profile of your entire business. You must reach consumers where they are now, which is online, as consumer behaviour has evolved.

Setting up your online presence requires:

1. Create an expert website: Websites are necessary for all businesses. If you don't already have one, you can easily create one yourself or hire someone to do it for you.

2. Retain and target clients on social media: Focus on the

platforms that are most used by your target market rather than being active on every social media platform. To prevent someone else from using your name, you should still sign up for all the other websites.

HOW DO YOU DRIVE TRAFFIC TO YOUR ONLINE BRAND?

1: Ensure that you are currently with all internet directories.

2. Increase business traffic using search engine optimization

3. Use internet reviews to attract more customers

4. Benefit from ad retargeting

5. Use content to increase brand recognition

CHAPTER 6

Developing an Interesting Brand Story

Every retail business owner has a tale to tell, whether it's about how they got started, why they chose this line of work, or how they converted a hobby into a successful enterprise. These stories intertwine to form a brand story.

There are other people who need to hear that tale than you. It strikes a chord with both your staff and consumers, building a community of brand defenders who stick by and defend it.

The effectiveness of storytelling is also supported by research. Not only do our brains comprehend tales, but also the human emotions they reflect. We are able to empathise when we comprehend the ideas and feelings of another.

This fosters genuine emotional ties that may lead to trust and, ultimately, financial success. Because of this, it's essential to understand how to create a brand story that is exclusive to you and your business.
A captivating narrative explaining how and why your

brand behaves the way it does is known as a brand story. It narrates the history, principles, objectives, and mission of your business.

This narrative establishes the context for all of your brand's interactions with customers, both in-person and online.

Brand storytelling is crucial because it allows you to connect with customers, build brand loyalty and trust, and differentiate your company from the competition. All of these things may lead to increased sales.

How to convey the tale of your brand

1. Decide on your why: Always start your brand narrative with the reason why you do what you do.

2. Recognize your product: To fully appreciate your brand's narrative, you must comprehend where and how your product fits inside it. A brand story that is unrelated to your product may result in an enthusiastic following but little sales.

3. Recognize your audience: Knowing your audience can help you create a great brand story. Knowing your target demographic is the third thing to

keep in mind while starting your brand narrative. It might be easier to understand how your brand narrative fits into their life if you are aware of their hobbies and problems.

4. Be succinct and straightforward.
It might be challenging to communicate the tales that are dearest to us. Why? Because we can become engrossed in minutiae we believe to be significant, but which may really undermine our main point.

Think of yourself as a sculptor beginning with an unformed piece of marble as you compress and refine it. The final product becomes more distinct—and memorable—as you eliminate more.

5. Emphasise human stories: People relate to people, not things or businesses. Instead of focusing on things, share human tales to develop a captivating origin narrative that increases brand loyalty.

CHAPTER 7

Utilising Social Media to Connect with Your Audience

Connecting with your consumers is a problem you must conquer if you want your business to succeed. This is where social media can assist; by using the correct strategy and channels, you can engage your target market more deeply and make them feel valued and loved by your company.

1. Reply to Consumer Messages: If you manage a company's social media, keep in mind that

you should constantly reply to customer comments and messages, whether they are favourable or unfavourable.

2. Start a Community Group: Community groups are one of the best methods to interact with your target audience on social media. While sometimes posting about your products or divulging insider knowledge is OK, the community group should mostly serve as a forum for your consumers to interact with one another and exchange ideas.

3. Run giveaways: Raffles is a great method to interact with your audience. People adore getting free stuff, and many

would be ready to share articles and tales about your business in exchange for entry.

4. Share Content That Isn't Just About Business: People follow brands on social media because they like the goods or services they offer, but not all of the content you share on your company's social media channels needs to be solely business-related. Post content that engages and motivates sharing from your target audience. You may, for instance, invite your followers to submit their favourite gift they've ever gotten throughout the holidays.

CHAPTER 8

Making the Most of Influencers to Promote Your Brand

Influencer marketing works because of what? It's comparable to how customers feel about suggestions from people in their own network. Because influencers have audiences who trust them, influencer marketing appears real in my opinion. These suggestions are perceived as a natural part of the influencer's content flow by the proper audience, which consists of your target persona. This isn't a sales pitch or a commercial, thus it's far more personal to the consumer and fosters brand loyalty through an honest medium.

Decide Which Influencers Are Best For Your Brand

It takes time and effort to find and engage with influencers that appeal to your audience since finding the proper influencers is not a quick and simple process. To aid your ideal target audience in making judgments about what to buy, uncover influencers that are linked to your brand's identities and who they will trust and identify with.

Start by looking for people that not only have a sizable fan base but also align with your customer profiles and their objectives. Study the material of prospective influencers and the kinds of comments that they get from followers to determine how engaged those people are and how they respond to those people. Are their supporters seeking recommendations and advice? Do they receive the information they require from these influencers to proceed with their decision-making process? If so, you should target influencers like them to raise awareness of your business.

How To Reach Your Buyer Personas Using Influencer Marketing

Utilising influencer marketing to get your audience's attention is the next step once you have discovered and begun networking with industry influencers. Here are methods to use your new influencer marketing plan to its full potential.

1. Marketing with shareable material: A smart place to start is by having your internal marketing team create some shareable content, such as succinct video clips, infographics, eye-catching photos, or informative articles.

Ask your influencers for advice on what they think will appeal to their audience the most.

2. Social media: Provide product samples or freebies to influencers and send them enough pertinent information about your product or service to enable them to produce their own social media content.

3. Video Marketing: To increase brand awareness, use influencers in your video marketing campaigns by placing them in the spotlight alongside your goods or services.

CHAPTER 9

Building Relationships at Networking Events

Any business or individual seeking to increase the reach of their services must-attend networking events. After all, developing strong connections with the appropriate individuals is the best method to increase business prospects.

Given its importance in establishing corporate relationships, networking events are now taking place all over the world. Whatever your area of expertise, there is undoubtedly a networking event that you will like and that will link you with the individuals you want to get in touch with.

However, it's crucial to know how to utilise these opportunities more than just attending networking events.

Building Relationships In Networking Events Requires

1. Get yourself ready in advance: Contrary to popular belief, you should start networking much before the event begins. You should begin planning for an event as soon as you confirm your attendance at it. Establish your objectives for the

networking event before anything else.

2. Put more emphasis on developing connections than attempting to sell:
Keep in mind that first impressions matter! Nobody appreciates being approached only with the intention of making a sale without even asking if you are interested. So avoid making this error! Although networking may be an effective sales tactic, you shouldn't go to a networking event expecting to make a quick sale.

3. Select your connections carefully:

It's important to manage your time well if you want to perform well at a networking event. Every second counts while you're at these events. Therefore, try to avoid wasting any of your time communicating with individuals that are irrelevant to your business and what you are attempting to achieve.

Concentrate on the people and organisations that can in some way assist you in extending your company opportunities and market reach.

4. Remember to do an efficient follow-up:
It's time to capitalise on your presence once the networking event has over. Establish a long-term relationship with the contacts you established at the event to help you achieve this. The best method to convert these connections into potential consumers for your company is to do an efficient follow-up.

CHAPTER 10

Conclusion

Building a strong brand is essential for any company or person trying to thrive in today's crowded and competitive market, as you have learned throughout this book. Your brand is the culmination of all of your interactions and experiences with your consumers and goes beyond just a logo or phrase. It is the way that others view and feel about your business or personal brand, and it has a big bearing on how successful you are.

It's crucial to concentrate on a few key aspects in order to develop a powerful brand. Establish your brand's personality and values first. What distinguishes your brand? What do you believe in? You may build a solid foundation for all of your branding activities by stating your brand's principles explicitly.

Spend money creating a distinctive brand identity next. This entails creating a logo and other branding materials that are aesthetically appealing, as well as selecting the appropriate color scheme and typefaces to express the personality of your company. Design is a crucial part of your entire branding strategy, so don't undervalue its effectiveness in creating a powerful brand.

Creating an online presence is crucial for creating a strong brand. This entails developing a professional website, participating in social media on a regular basis, and producing high-caliber content that highlights the skills and personality of your company. You may further improve the exposure and reach of your brand by cultivating connections with influencers and business titans.

Finally, don't forget to set your brand out from the competitors.

Find the selling factors that set you apart from the competition and make advantage of them. Showcase your brand's personality and beliefs via personal branding and narrative, and don't be afraid to experiment and be creative.

Consistency is key as you attempt to develop your brand. Strive to consistently provide outstanding customer service while maintaining consistent messaging and visual identity across all channels. Analyze your brand's performance using data and analytics to guide your branding strategy selections.

You can create a powerful, distinctive brand that stands out in a competitive market and draws devoted clients by using the advice in this article. Keep in mind that developing a brand is a constant process, so don't be afraid to adjust and evolve as your company does. You'll be well on your way to creating a brand that genuinely shines if you keep these guidelines in mind.

www.ingramcontent.com/pod-product-compliance
Lightning Source LLC
Chambersburg PA
CBHW050314220526
45465CB00005B/1985